2B

ANNE-MARIE BRECKON
E.C.E., B.A. Honors, B.Ed

E.C.E., Early Childhood Education Diploma,
B.A. Honors Bachelor of Arts History Degree,
B.Ed Bachelor of Education Degree,
O.C.T. Ontario College of Teachers
Jay Shetty Genius & Certified Coach

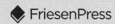 FriesenPress

Suite 300 - 990 Fort St
Victoria, BC, V8V 3K2
Canada

www.friesenpress.com

Copyright © 2020 by Anne-Marie Breckon
First Edition — 2020

All rights reserved.

No part of this publication may be reproduced in any form, or by any means, electronic or mechanical, including photocopying, recording, or any information browsing, storage, or retrieval system, without permission in writing from FriesenPress.

You never know how close you are, never give up on your dreams! Image original illustrator unknown.

Red Fox eyes photo courtesy of Jessica Kirste photography.

ISBN
978-1-5255-8148-9 (Hardcover)
978-1-5255-8149-6 (Paperback)
978-1-5255-8150-2 (eBook)

Distributed to the trade by The Ingram Book Company

DEDICATED TO MY BIG SISTER DEE-ANNE. AND FOR ZAK.
MAY YOU BE HELD IN LOVING LIGHT ENERGY.

Just breathe! In French, we say *inspire et expire*.

Controlling your breathing is something that you already do. Think about the last time you were running. You automatically adjusted your breathing and began pacing your breath to enable you to run. Scientists say that when you control your breathing, you can control your mind. You can calm your mind using breathing exercises. Try these now, and find the one you like best.

Breathe in for a count of four, and breathe out for a count of four. Repeat two more times.

Now try breathing in while you move your left ear to touch your left shoulder. Breathe out and position your head straight. Now breathe in and move your right ear to your right shoulder. Breathe out and position your head straight. Try repeating these three more times.

How do you feel now? What did you think of this exercise?

FAMOUS FAILURES

EVERYONE FAILS SOMETIMES. In order 2B good at something, you will likely fail many times before you succeed. Google the name of a famous person you admire, plus the word failure. It's likely that before they were successful, they failed. Learning the lesson, or what you can do differently the next time, is what makes you a success. A winner is just a loser who got up and tried one more time. Remember that failure is an event, not a person. When you learn the lesson, then you have in fact succeeded. Einstein said, "Everyone is a genius, but if you judge a fish by its ability to climb a tree, it will spend its whole life feeling stupid."

The best thing you can do is to nurture your own inner light. Be your genuine, authentic self. Some people will judge you and not like you anyway. When you are true to yourself, the right people will love you! Each individual person is unique. You are the only person who can be you! Nurture your natural talents and abilities, and use them in service to others in the world. One of the expressions I've coined is, "We are all human beings, and that is why we are all equal." None of us are perfect. Perfection is a myth! Be the best YOU that you can be, and don't compare yourself to someone else's selfie.

"Have you Filled a Bucket Today" is a book written by Carol McCloud. I like the way it illustrates that each person has their own bucket of happiness. First, your bucket needs to be full for you. What overflows is for you to give to everyone else. The only way to fill your bucket is to nurture yourself, and show kindness to others.

Doing things that are good for you, or that make you feel good, are acts of self-love. Mine include; yoga, meditation, nature walks, reading and writing. What are yours?

My self-love habits are: _____ ,

_____ , _____ .

Try to do at least one every day.

Small changes make a big difference over time.

> $1.00 today is not very much. $1.00 every day, over the course of a week, is $7.00. A dollar a day over a year is $365.00. That sure does add up! Keep practicing the strategies that work for you to help you to have a healthy and happy life ☺.

A **fixed mindset** is the inability to broaden your intellectual horizons. A **growth mindset** is being open to new experiences and continuing to try.

Having a growth mindset is a winning mindset!

Try to do more of what makes you happy. Living in a state of love and light is the ideal goal. Your headspace determines everything. Clearing your mind, and practicing mindfulness and meditation, can help you to have a good headspace. Focusing on the *feeling* of abundance can also help. Like training a muscle, you must practice feeling good. Holding on to moments and feelings of joy and love will help you rewire your brain. The ultimate assessment is, are you able 2B alone peacefully when you are unplugged and alone with your mind?

List 3 things you like doing or things that make you happy.

_____

_____

_____

Try to do these things as often as you can.

This is Simba's happy place. He loves being in nature.
@Simba_thebestboy on Instagram.

Where are you when you are happy? Take a few seconds now. Close your eyes, and try to picture a place or a memory where you were happy. What are you doing? What do you see? The more details you can visualize, the better. Try to create a space in your mind using a memory or a place. Then think of this place when you need a happy thought.

One of my happy places is found in nature. I envision being on a trail in natural surroundings, outdoors and by the water. I also use memories from music concerts. When I get stressed, I breathe and think of the feeling of being in that happy space.

Where is your happy place? _____

What does it smell like? _____

What are you doing? _____

What do you see? _____

What do you feel? _____

What do you hear? _____

Now try closing your eyes and picturing yourself there. Really *feel* what it is like to be there.

INTERNAL DIALOGUE

WHAT IS YOUR INTERNAL DIALOGUE? Sometimes, when things are not going as well as we would like them to, we become engaged in negative self-talk. Dr. Daniel Amen is a brain doctor who studies the effects of negative self-talk on your brain. He takes pictures of his clients' brains using a SPECT scan, and he can see the damage internal dialogue can do to your brain flow and function.

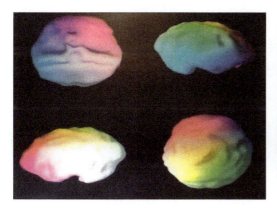
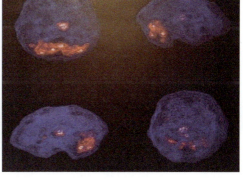

Dr Amen takes SPECT Images of the brain. *This image shows blood flow and brain activity.*

He created the **ANT** strategy to help you have a healthy brain. Dr. Amen says **ANT**s are **automatic negative thoughts**. Ask yourself, "Is this thought true? Is it really true?" and "What else can I do instead?" He wrote a book called, "Captain Snout and the Superpower Questions," which is a brilliant story that explains his ANT strategy.

The next time you are thinking negative thoughts, catch yourself doing it. Then stop and record your thoughts on a device, or write them out on a piece of paper. Reread or replay it. While you listen, ask yourself, "Would I say this to someone I love, like my friend or my mom?" If the answer is no, then keep working on the strategy. Start to identify when you are having the negative thought and try swapping it for a more positive thought.

3S SPOT, STOP, SWAP

Try to spot that you are speaking negatively to yourself, stop it, and swap it with the most positive thought you can think of. Draw a symbol in the box below to represent spot, stop, and swap.

SPOT	STOP	SWAP

Fill in the blank to finish the sentence. "I get to _____."

When you "get to" do something, it is usually always something you really like and really want to do. For example, "I get to go to Canada's Wonderland."

Brain scientists know that there are chemicals like dopamine, oxytocin, serotonin, and endorphins that contribute to the pleasure centres in your brain. There are things that you can do that will increase the release of these chemicals. Each person is unique; what works for one person may not work for someone else. It is up to you to identify the activities you like to do to help release these chemicals. Some examples include: painting, dancing, music, writing, sports, mechanics, gardening, cooking, and creating.

Name 3 things that you enjoy doing. Do these as often as you can to help release the happiness chemicals in your brain.

1 _____

2 _____

3 _____

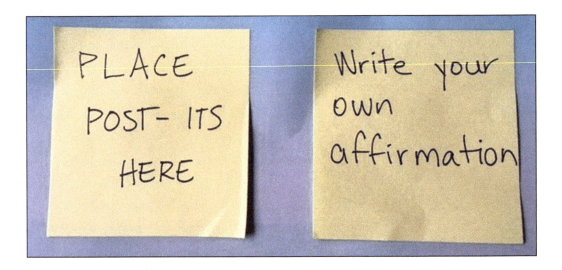

Affirmations are a powerful tool for self-growth. Keep them simple and focused on what you want to have happen. Write it out on a piece of paper (or a post-it™), then attach it to your wall and look at it often. Using your affirmations as your screen saver is another idea.

Repeat your affirmations out loud or to yourself, in the mornings and before bed.

When writing affirmations follow these simple steps.

- Keep it positive (reword it to avoid the use of the word not).
- Keep it focused on what you do want.
- Keep at it. The longer you work on it the better. Just like when you lift weights and develop muscles, small changes add up over time.

- "This is amazing, I am so grateful, what's next?"
- "You are what you think about."
- "People are loving and kind."

These are a few affirmations currently written on brightly colored paper and posted around my home. Do they work? Try it yourself and see.

I had been sending out the affirmation, "People are loving and kind." Then one day while I was driving home from work, I spotted a fox at the side of the road. The fox was alive, but couldn't physically drag itself up off the curb after being hit by a car. It touched my heart, and I just couldn't leave it there to die. I turned my car around to go back and help. As I turned around, that little voice of fear in my head was saying, "Come on Anne-Marie, what are you going to do? Pull out your magical fox experience?" But I faced my fear and did it anyway.

I parked in front of the fox. Another woman had also stopped to help, and she had a Rubbermaid bin. I put on my car's hazard lights for safety. The lights ensured that cars would have to go around the fox and the women at the side of the road. Safety, and a Rubbermaid bin…

Just then, another woman approached. She parked behind the fox, and she had a towel. So there we were: three women, two cars, a towel, and a Rubbermaid bin.

I spoke in a reassuring tone to the fox, attempting to calm it. Obviously, it didn't understand human, but it did understand loving kindness and that it need not be fearful. Its little heart was visibly beating intensely fast against its soft, orange fur. The fox's fear was obvious. I was totally present in the moment when I was standing at the side of the road staring into the eyes of this scared little fox.

As we three women stood around the fox discussing what to do first, a police cruiser pulled over to investigate. The two male officers exited their car. Traffic was backing up, but was moving slowly. The older of the officers questioned us. Had we seen who had hit the fox? Was it one of us? The fox was likely suffering from a broken back. The visible road marks on its legs were bloody. "Veterinarians won't operate on wild animals," he said. Then he conceded. Perhaps he identified that we three women were determined to rescue this fox.

The police officer indicated that he had a pair of rubber gloves in the trunk of his cruiser, and the younger officer retrieved them. I held the Rubbermaid bin. The bin owner held the lid.

The older officer used the gloves to toss the towel onto the fox, then picked it up. He placed the fox in the bin, I rotated it, and the other woman put the lid on.

The bin, with the fox in it, was placed in the back of the bin woman's car. She was with an older female relative who had stayed in the vehicle. She had been calling wildlife sanctuaries, and she found one that would help the fox. I drove away, incredulous. I came home and recounted the story to my daughter, Katey. As much as it was unbelievable, it was an example of "people are loving and kind." The affirmation that I was currently focused on.

Using affirmations, and a lot of my other knowledge, comes from studying. Yes, I am a teacher, but I am also always a student. I love learning, especially when I get to pick the subject and how I approach it. My biggest mentor in life is Jay Shetty. He is a former monk whose intention is to "Make Wisdom Go Viral." He taught me about affirmations and the spot, stop, swap strategy. He has a majestic voice when he says the words, "Balance, calm, ease, stillness, and peace" during his live mediations and growth sessions in the Genius community.

The best thing you can ever do is to love yourself, and 2B grateful for what you do have. Here's a secret: when we focus on all the things we do not have or do not want; we just get more of it. Instead, focus on exactly what you do want.

GRATITUDE

· · · · · · ·

GRATITUDE is another way to increase your well-being. Be grateful for what you do have, and you will attract more of it. Focus on the feeling of being genuinely grateful. Try this **TY5** strategy. Look around you right now, and say, "Thank you," out loud, for five things. "Thank you for my bed, thank you for my book, thank you for a warm shower, thank you for healthy food, thank you for clean clothes."

TY1 _____,

TY2 _____,

TY3 _____,

TY4 _____,

TY5 _____

VISUALIZATION

VISUALIZATION is a tool that can help you to focus on what you want.

In your mind, picture what you want, or what you want to have happen. Hold this image in your mind. Think of it often. Describe it.

_____

_____

_____

Hold an image in your mind of what you want. Think about how it feels, and imagine yourself having it or doing it. Here's a real-life example. Imagine approaching an intersection in a car. The light is green, but you want to make it through the intersection before the light turns red. You can say, "Stay green" or you can say, "Don't turn red." Try visualizing yourself in a car approaching an intersection. Say, "stay green, stay green, stay green." What does that make you feel, or what mood does that set?

- Now visualize yourself approaching an intersection and saying, "Don't turn red, don't turn red, don't turn red." In this scenario you are focusing on "turn red," which is the opposite of what you want to have happen. Mother Teresa said, "Do not invite me to an anti-war rally, as you are focused on war. Invite me to a peace rally, and I'm there!" She knew the power of words.

- Another strategy is to make a vision board. This is as simple as using a piece of paper and putting images on it of things you would like to have. This helps you to focus on what you do want.

- Controlling your breathing can help in any situation. Try deep breathing from your stomach. Breathe in for a count of five and out for a count of two. Repeat twice more.

- Another breathing method is the four, five, six count. Try breathing in for a count of four, holding for a count of five, and breathing out for a count of six. Repeat three times.

Things happen in life that can cause stress. Your reaction to it, and how you deal with it, is your only superpower. Some of the major stressors in life are moving, illness, divorce, unemployment, imprisonment, and death. Stress levels go up and down over the course of your lifetime. Learning stress management strategies that work for you will be beneficial for you throughout your life. These tools can help you manage your feelings during more stressful or anxiety provoking times.

Anxiety is a normal emotion experienced by all humans at some point in their life.

Google dictionary says that, "Anxiety is a feeling of worry, nervousness, or unease, typically about an imminent event or something with an uncertain outcome." During periods of increased anxiety, try grounding strategies like **5S**enses. Think about something you can touch, taste, smell, see, and hear. Repeat as necessary.

5S

Name something you can

SMELL	
SEE	
HEAR	
TOUCH	
TASTE	

Other helpful techniques when experiencing anxiety include attempting to put things into perspective. Asking yourself questions like, "Will this make a difference five years from now?" can help to determine the value you should place on this particular event or situation. Another strategy is rating things on a scary scale. Jay Shetty taught me about the Scary Scale. You rate all of the things that scare you on a scale of 1-100, on a number line. Seeing them visually like that can allow you to put things in perspective.

Plot situations or things you worry about on the Scary Scale below. Rate them between one and 100 based on how scary they might be, with one being not very scary and 100 being very scary.

NOT SO SCARY   SCARIEST

1 ································· 50 ································· 100

Sometimes the things we worry about never happen. But sometimes, things in life are way scarier than usual. Talking to a trusted adult can help. KidsHelpPhone has a trusted adult available 24 hours a day, 7 days a week. Someone is always there if you need to talk. Call them at 1-800-668-6868, or go online at www.kidshelpphone.ca. Sometimes people do not always say or show us they love us as often as they should, talking to a neutral adult professional can be helpful.

In the 1980's, Terry Fox ran across Canada on one leg. He knew how to break big things into smaller pieces. He focused on running to the next streetlight, the next mile marker. Chunking and breaking big things into smaller pieces, then handling one small piece at a time, is very helpful. What is one simple step you can take? What can you do next?

The **Terry Fox strategy.** Think of something BIG and try breaking it down into smaller pieces.

SOMETHING BIG	ONE SMALL PIECE	ONE SMALL PIECE	ONE SMALL PIECE	ONE SMALL PIECE

Try to do just one of the small pieces. Then the next. Then the next. Then the next.

Dr. Daniel Amen says that there are seven different types of Attention Deficit Disorder (A.D.D.). Attention Deficit Hyperactivity Disorder (A.D.H.D) is one of the seven types. People with A.D.D. may have a hard time falling asleep at night, as it may be hard to shut down the activity in your brain.

Even without A.D.D., most people will experience this at least once in their life. Sleep is one of the major contributors to your well-being. It is the way that the human body heals and resets itself. Most people need seven or eight hours a night, while young people need ten or more. The best advice is to sleep in a place that is as cave-like as possible. In order to have a room that is as cave like as possible, remove any devices that emit a glow or a sound from your room. It is helpful to go to bed at the same time every night and have a night time routine.

Sleep is one of the most important parts of your health. Getting ready for bed like brushing your teeth and putting on your pyjamas is part of a bedtime *routine*. Describe your bedtime routine.

_____
_____

What could you do to improve your bedtime routine?

_____
_____

When you get into bed, try thinking of all the things that went right that day. Ask yourself, "What went well today?" Then mentally create a list in your mind of everything that was good about the day. If something didn't go well and you are worried about it, think about the scenario with the ending you would rather have had.

If you are worried about something that is going to happen tomorrow, try writing it out, or thinking through your intentions for the next day. That means thinking it through with the outcome you would like to have. For example, let's say you have to give a presentation and you are nervous about it. Set your intention to have a successful presentation where you speak clearly and everything goes well. Then forget about it.

Using the breathing strategies and the TY5 strategy, and counting backwards and forwards to 100, may help you sleep as well. Sometimes white noise like a fan or nature sounds may be helpful.

If you are constantly not sleeping soundly, perhaps talk to your doctor about going to a sleep clinic for an assessment.

FREQUENCY

What frequency are you at? When attempting to get a radio station, sometimes you will hear static, and you have to fine tune the buttons to make the song come in loud and clear. Just like a radio, you have an inner frequency that you vibrate at. If you are always happy, you are vibrating at a higher frequency. If you are always focused on the negative, or you are ill or tired, you are vibrating at a lower frequency. Ways to increase or change your frequency include moving your body and doing the things you love. Experiencing feelings of joy and love also helps to change your frequency.

Meditation and yoga are natural ways to increase your frequency. Neuroscientists are the scientists who study the brain. They have proven that meditation changes your brain waves or your brain frequency.

Magnetic Resonance Imaging (M.R.I.) shows picture proof that the amygdala, the "fight or flight" center of your brain, shrinks after meditation. The amygdala shrinking is a good thing. It is like a flexing of a muscle. The amygdala is responsible for your body's reaction to stress, and is associated with fear and emotion. While you meditate you are literally calming your brain. The activity in your brain slows down and reduces the flow of incoming information. It is normal for your mind to wander during meditation, you just have to keep bringing your thoughts back.

MEDITATION

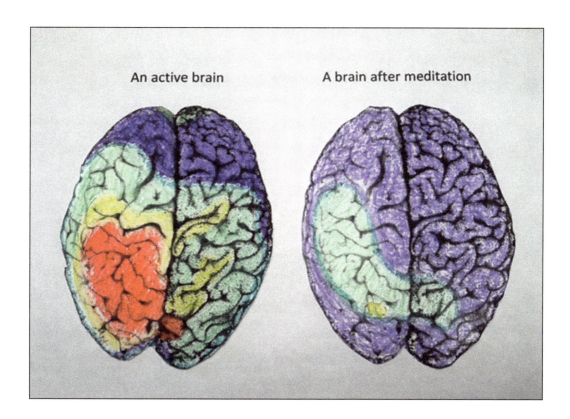

When grieving the death of a loved one or a pet, psychologists say that there are different stages of grief. I believe each stage of grief is unique to the person and the situation. The intensity of each, and the timing of going through each stage, varies based on each person.

Stages of grief include shock, denial, anger, guilt, and acceptance.

Time heals. The distance from the event reduces the rawness of it. Feel the emotions that come over you. Cry if you need to. Work through it. You will get there. Know your strategies for self-love and use them. Meditation. Me-time. Massage. Sports. Music. Nature. Exercise. Art. Do what works for you.

There is a big difference between being sad and being depressed. The Canadian Mental Health Association defines depression as lasting for a long period of time, and affecting many areas of your day-to-day life. Sadness is one of the symptoms of depression, and can last as long as any other mood. Depression is a clinical disorder that affects the brain and hormones. People suffering with depression may be at risk of suicide.

> My big sister died when she was sixteen and I was fourteen. It was a 100/100 on the scary scale. I felt all of the emotions listed above: shock, denial, anger, guilt, and eventually, acceptance. Sometimes I felt many of those feelings all at once. Grief felt like waves crashing over me. It felt like nothing would ever make it better, but I was able to find comfort with the passing of time and practicing self-love strategies. Eventually, the waves came less and less frequently.

> Our family found out afterwards that my sister was suffering from depression and had committed suicide. This was especially shocking given that in those days, mental health, depression, and suicide were not talked about. We had barely even heard the word "depression" before this happened. 21 years and a day later, a ten-year-old former student of mine also committed suicide. These two events made me realize the importance of mental health, and especially how important it is to be able to talk about it.

A wise monk said, "Suicide transfers the pain from the person who is suffering onto their loved ones." Your mom, dad, sister, brother, or anyone who loves you will spend the rest of their lives missing you. I know this 2B true. This is why suicide is not an option. If you are feeling this way, please get help. Talk it through with friends or family or a mental health professional, and know that you are not alone, and you will get through it. You impact so many lives, and may not even realize how much these people care about you.

> Remember the KidsHelpPhone I mentioned before? There is always someone there to listen. 1-800-668-6868 or www.kidshelpphone.ca. Talking to a trusted adult in your life can help as well. Finally, Mental Health Associations have professionals who are trained to help.

Most of the challenges you will face in life are temporary, only a single step on the journey of your life. Many of these challenges you won't even remember in five years, despite how daunting they may seem right now. Life is full of both great things and not so great things, and it's up to you to focus on which things you want to remember.

Appreciate the great things your life can offer you. Some of the best experiences in life are easy to forget about: how much you like watching the sunset; the way your best friend's laugh sounds; how your pet waits excitedly for you when you get home; how ice cream or a really good burger tastes; how good it feels to dance in the rain; the new album or song your favourite band is releasing; or how someday you could be an incredible artist or scientist or teacher or parent or whatever you want 2B.

Acknowledge that you are able to do what you love doing, are good enough to do it, and are worthy to do it. Follow your passions and live your life to its fullest. Whether that means pursuing a career or petting a dog, tomorrow is always a new day. It is a new beginning, and another chance to feel and give love to yourself and others.

The title of this book is 2B for a couple of different reasons. First, I consider 2B a root word, because you can put any word in front of it (prefix) and any word after it (suffix).

For example, "<u>got</u> 2B" and "2B <u>great</u>." Fill in your own prefix and suffix below.

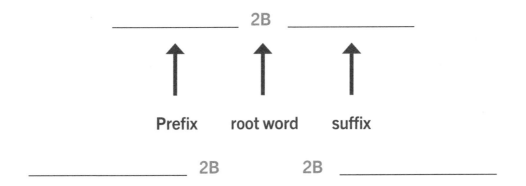

The second reason the title is 2B is because when I was in grade two, we had two classes, 2A and 2B. I was in 2B. It was then that I wrote, "Anne-Marie 2B" in the drawer in my mother's hutch. It is still there to this day, and I see it every time I open that drawer.

CPSIA information can be obtained
at www.ICGtesting.com
Printed in the USA
LVHW072337170121
676739LV00038B/1547